Fairy and Fantasy 3
Line Art Coloring Book
by Christine Karron

FAIRY and FANTASY 3
Line Art Coloring book by Christine Karron

First published July 2021

Copyright © 2021 Christine Karron
All rights reserved.

Other than for personal use or book review, no part of this book may
be reproduced or transmitted in any way, in whole or part,
without written permission from the copyright holder.

ISBN: 9798533355551
Imprint: Independently published

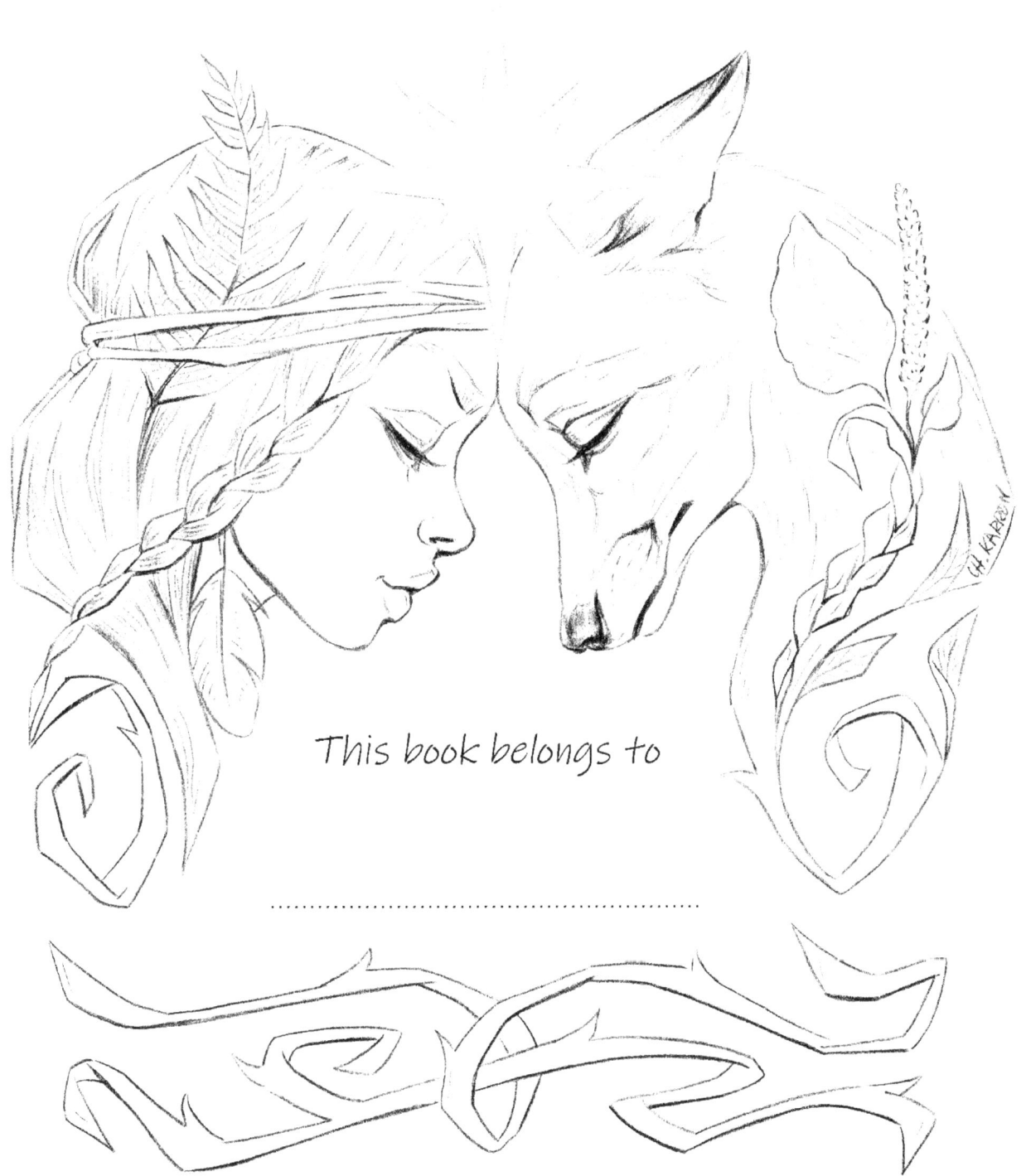

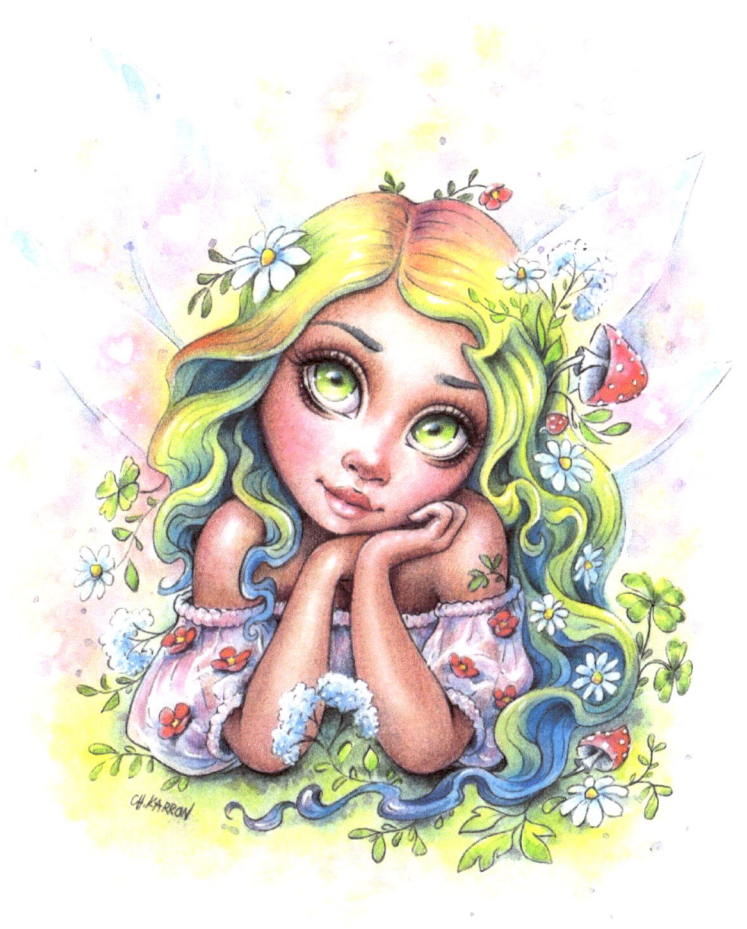

All illustrations in this book were originally created and traditionally hand drawn by the artist Christine Karron. For coloring inspirations, demo videos and more about Christine's artwork visit www.chkarron.com

This coloring book is suitable for all ages and all skill levels.
Recommended for coloring with markers, colored pencils,
pens and crayons. If using wet media, place a sheet of thick paper
or card stock behind the coloring page to prevent bleed through.

Fairy and Fantasy 3

1. Happy Fairy
2. Fairy Dust
3. Fairies with Fox Baby
4. Flora
5. Fairy Flower Bouquet
6. Frog Prince
7. Queen of the Seven Seas
8. Astral Fae
9. Fairy Besties
10. Star Catcher
11. Spring Awakening
12. Dreamy Fae
13. Dream Weaver
14. Fae Darling
15. Pearls of Life
16. Message in the Bottle
17. Flourish Fae
18. Fairy Flower Crown
19. Spring Wind
20. Sleeping Beauty
21. Helping Hands
22. Orchid Dream
23. Joys of Summer
24. Tarot Reader
25. Bonded

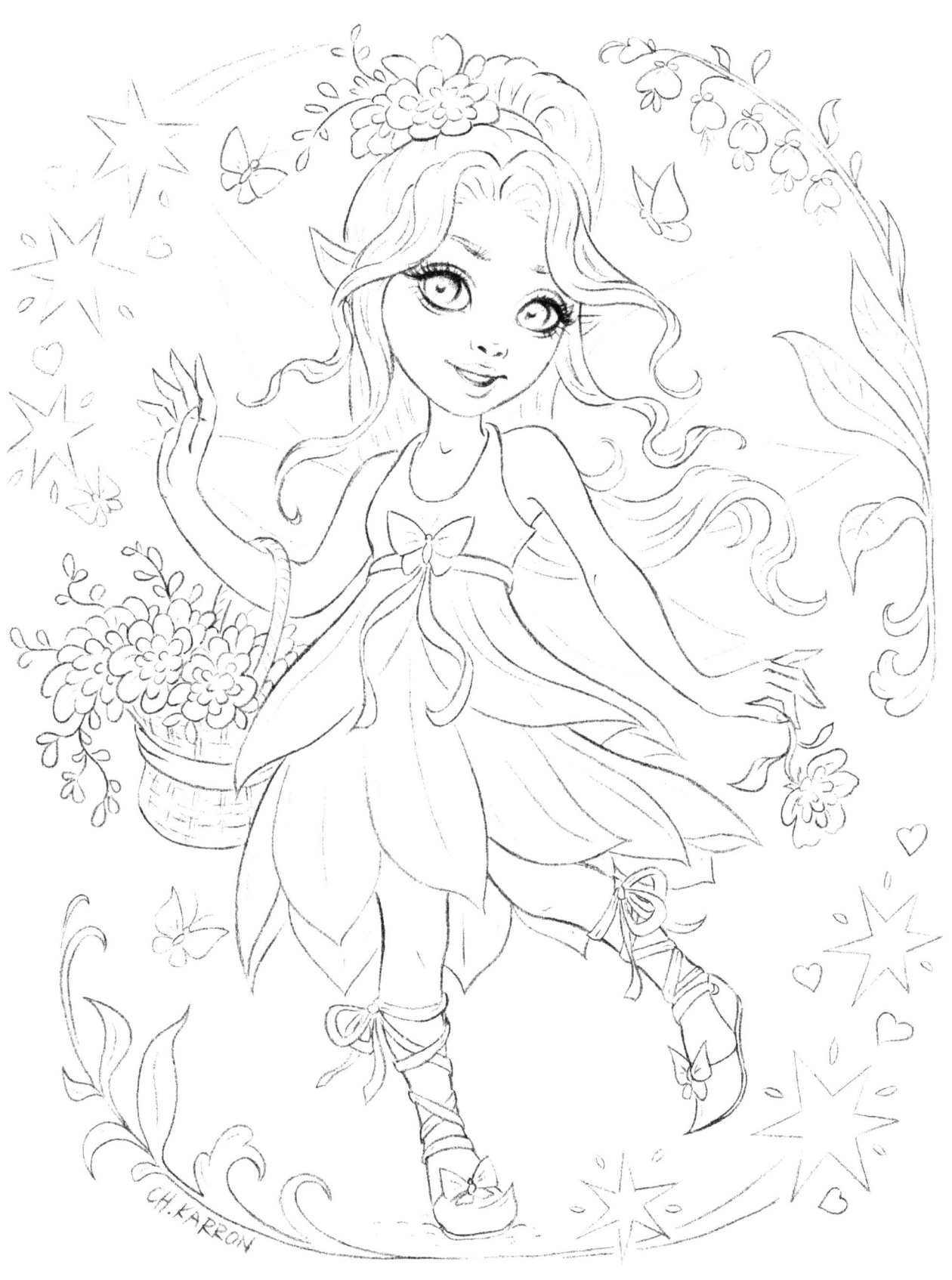

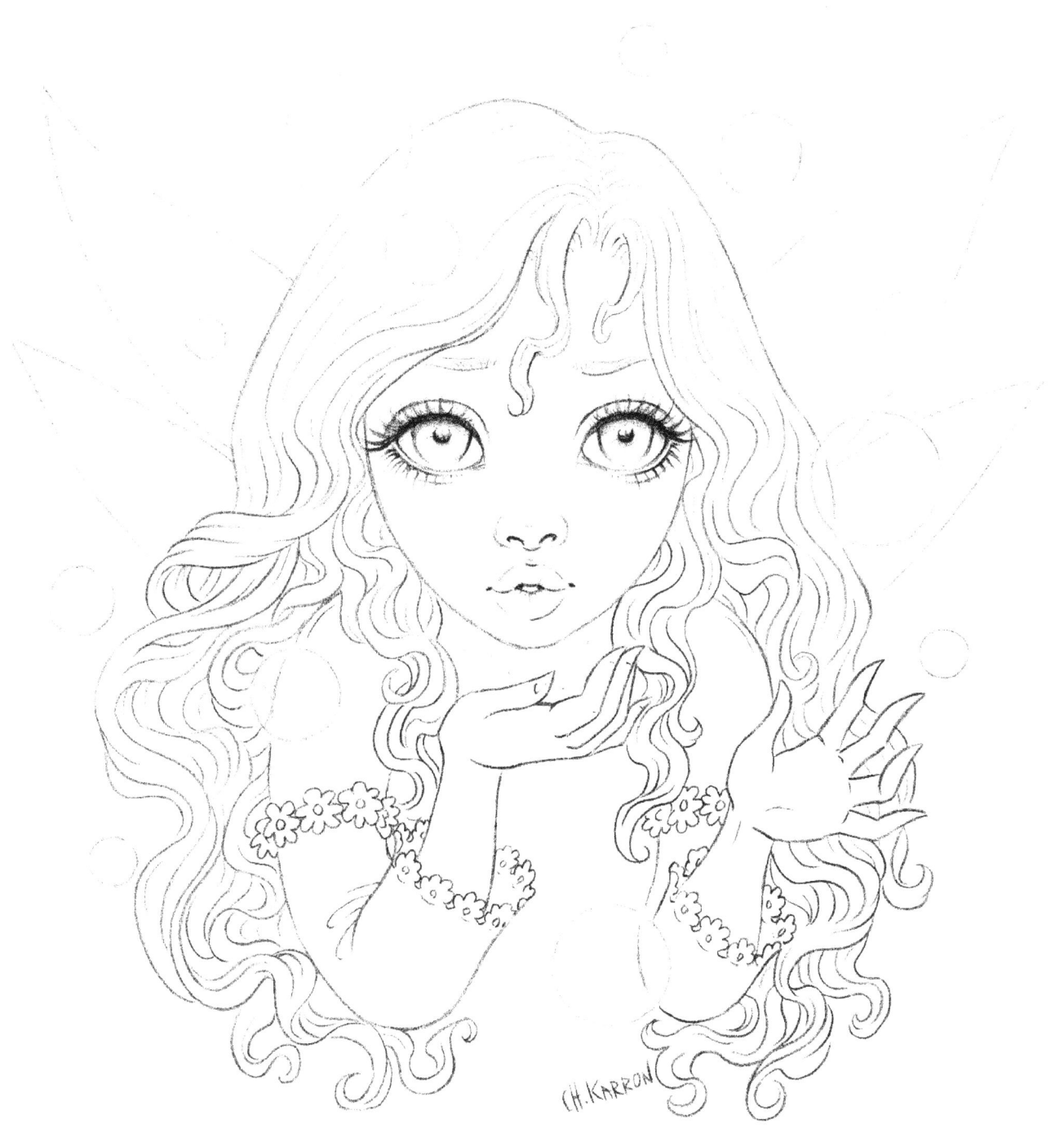

Fairy and Fantasy 3 © Christine Karron

Fairy Dust

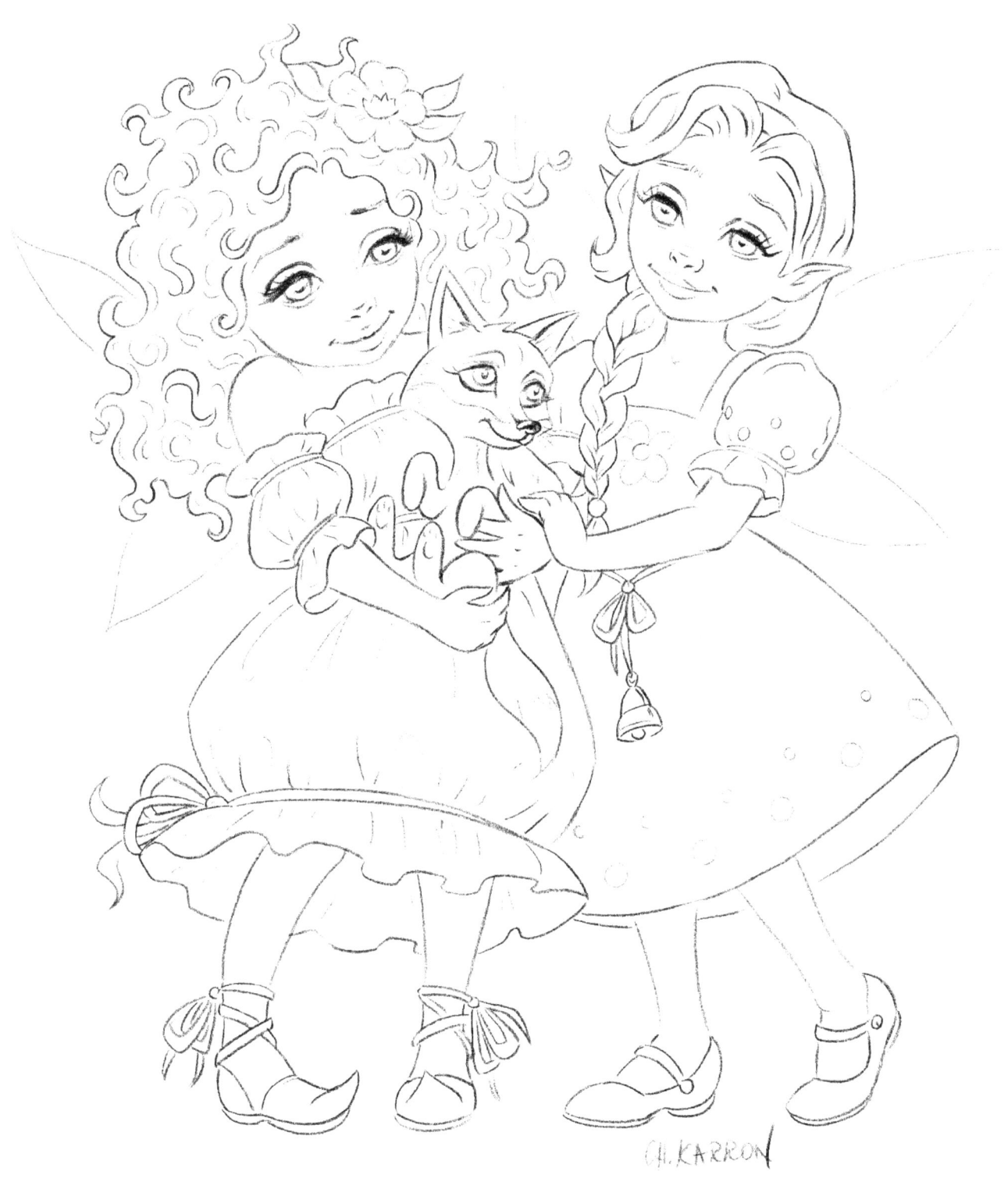

Fairy and Fantasy 3 © Christine Karron Fairies with Fox Baby

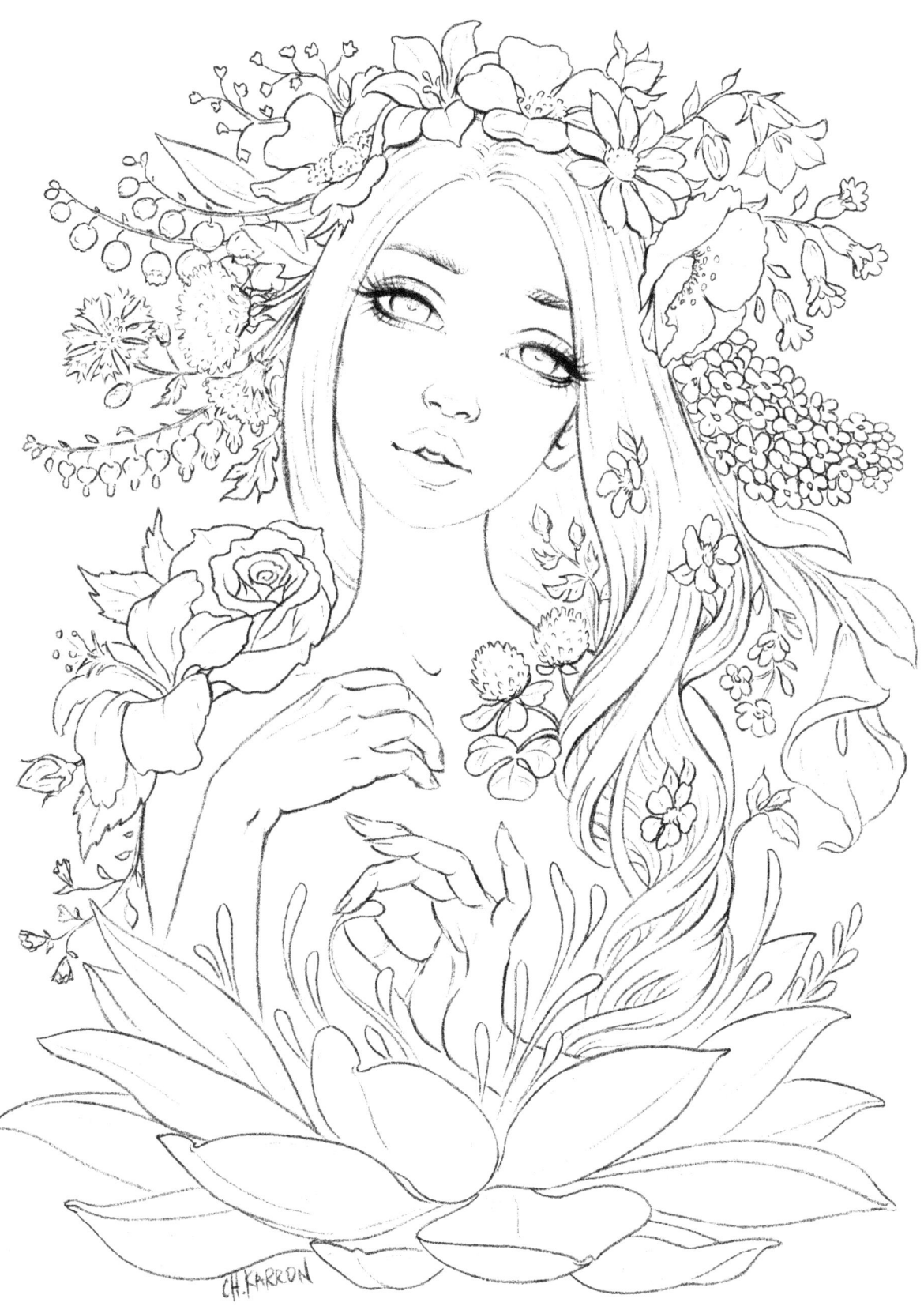

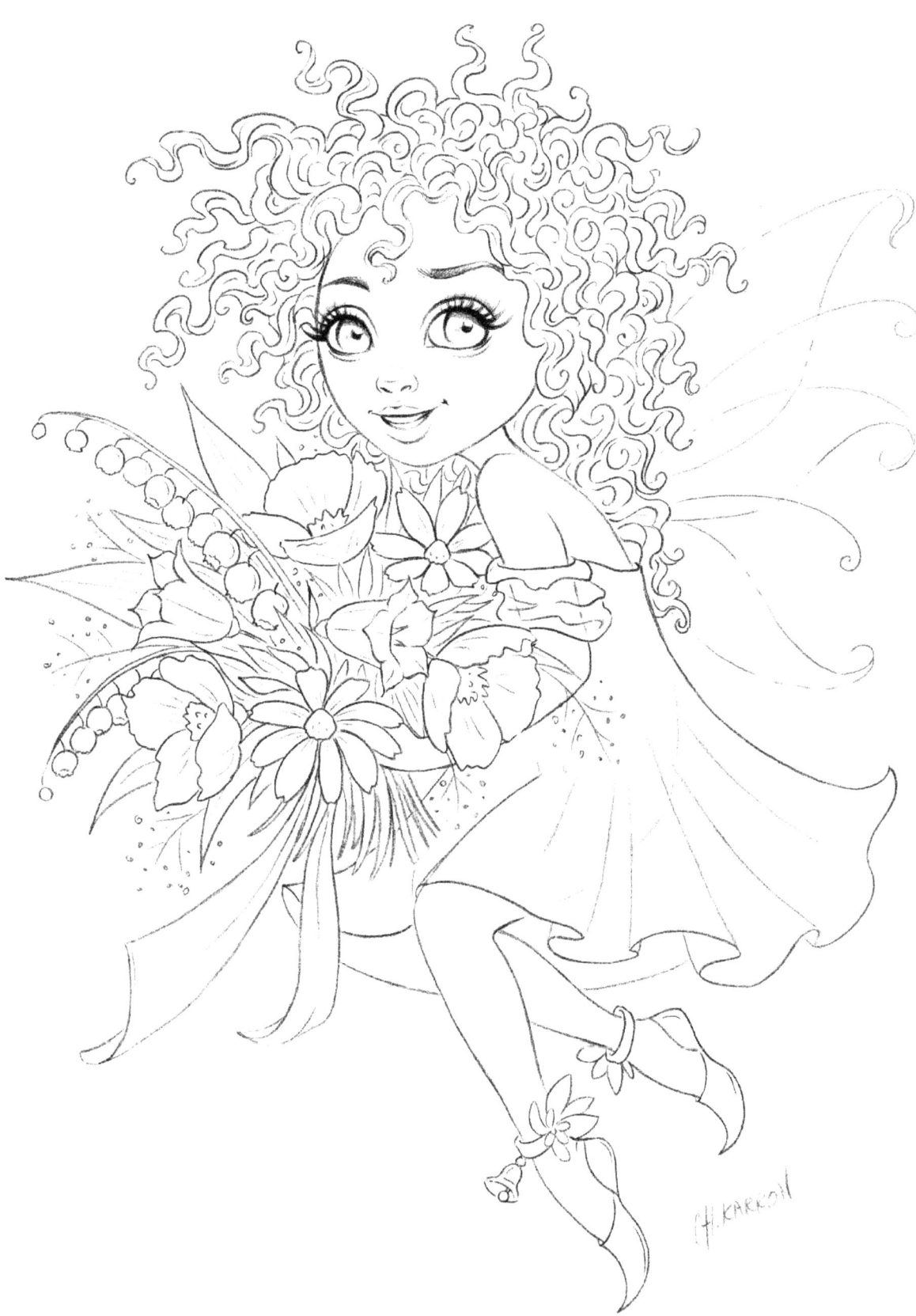

Fairy and Fantasy 3 © Christine Karron — Fairy Flower Bouquet

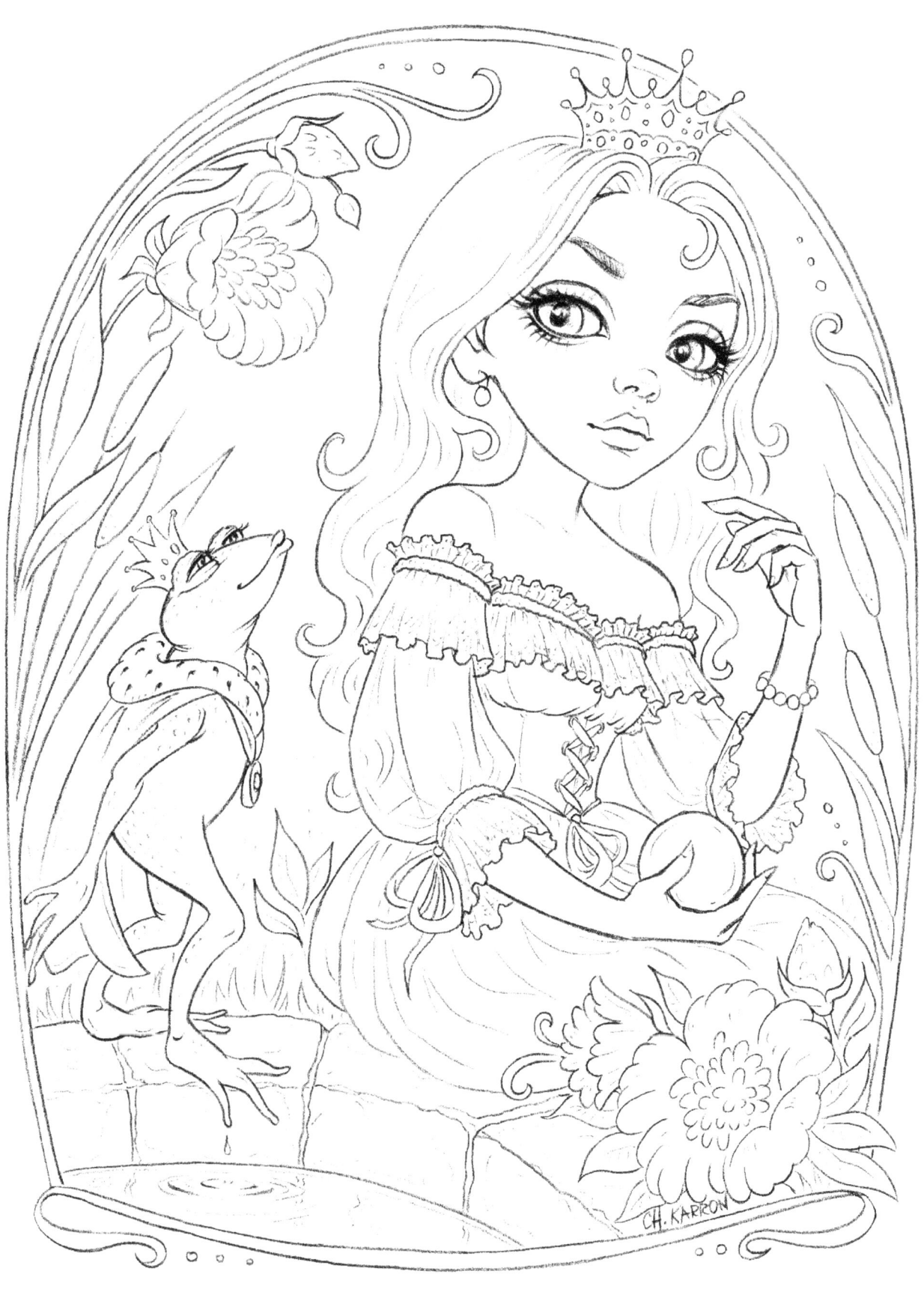

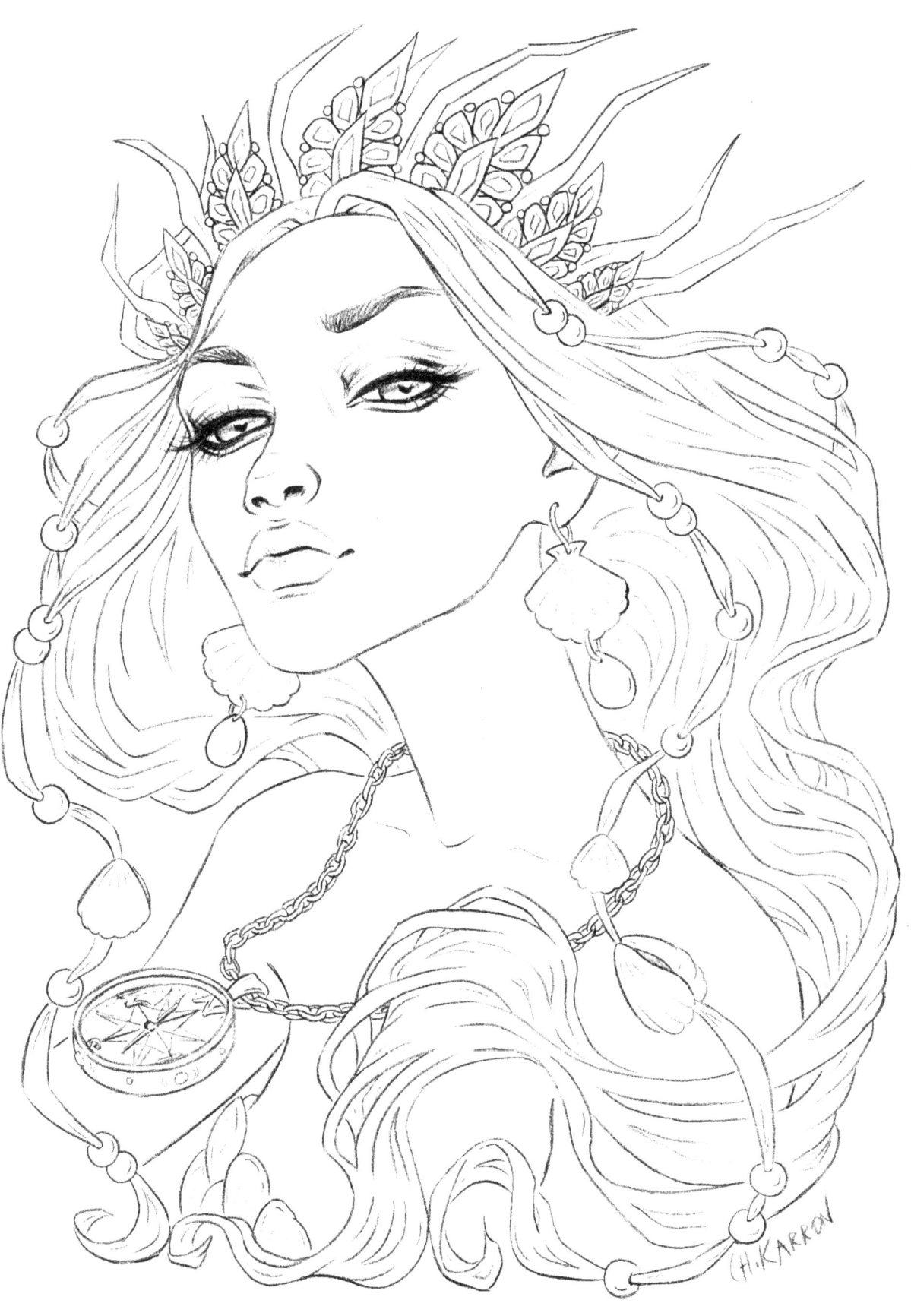

Fairy and Fantasy 3 © Christine Karron — Queen of the Seven Seas

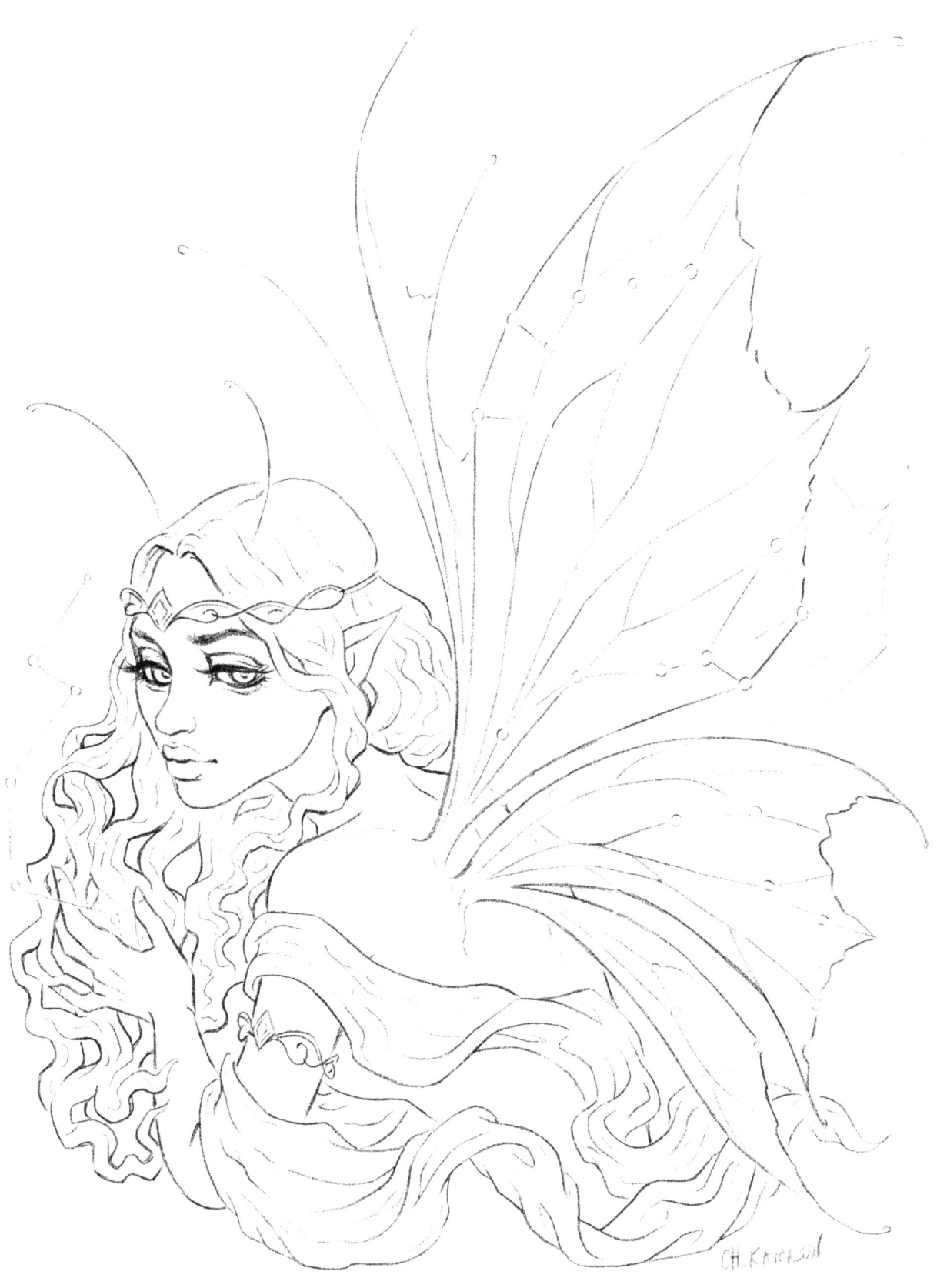

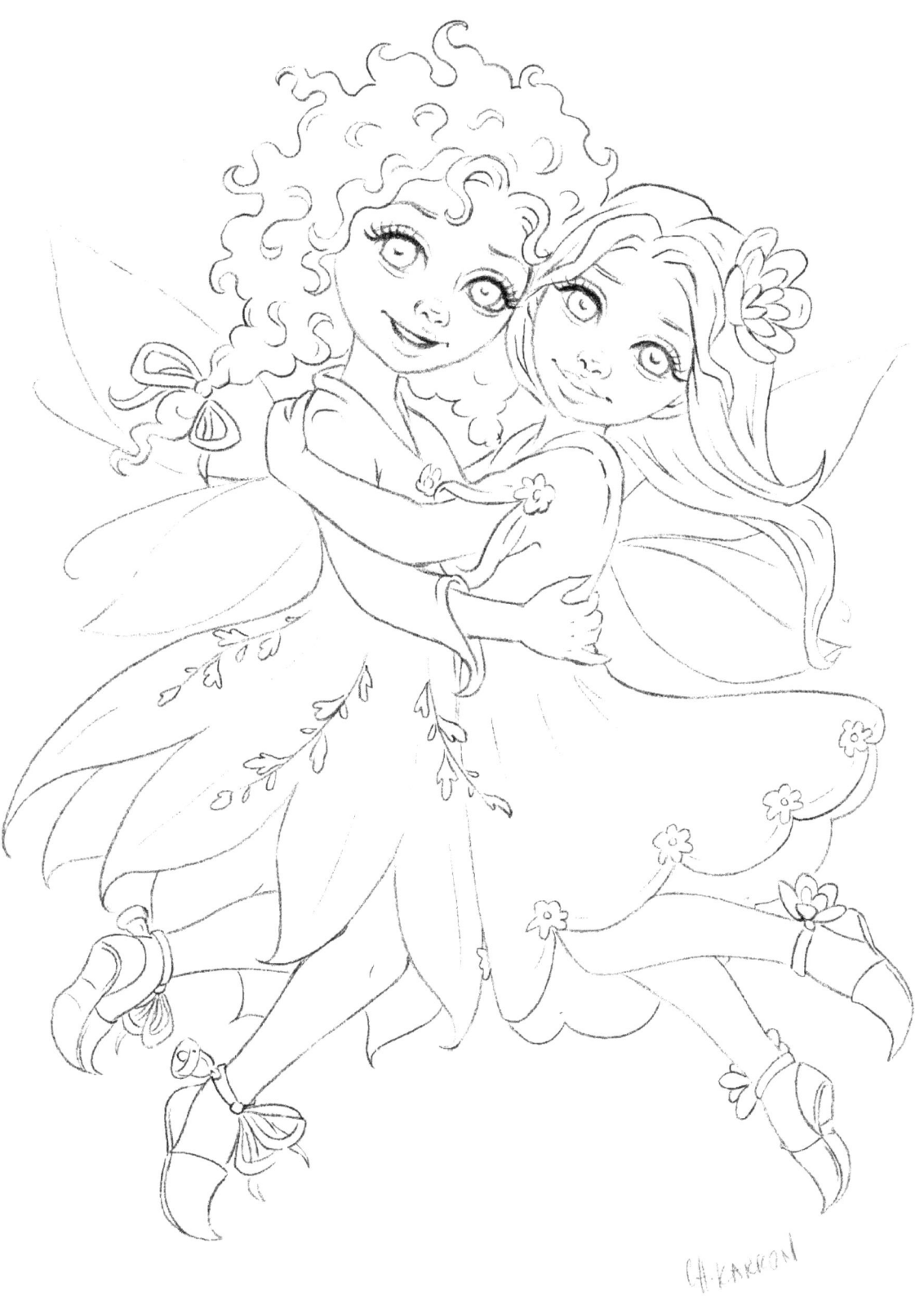

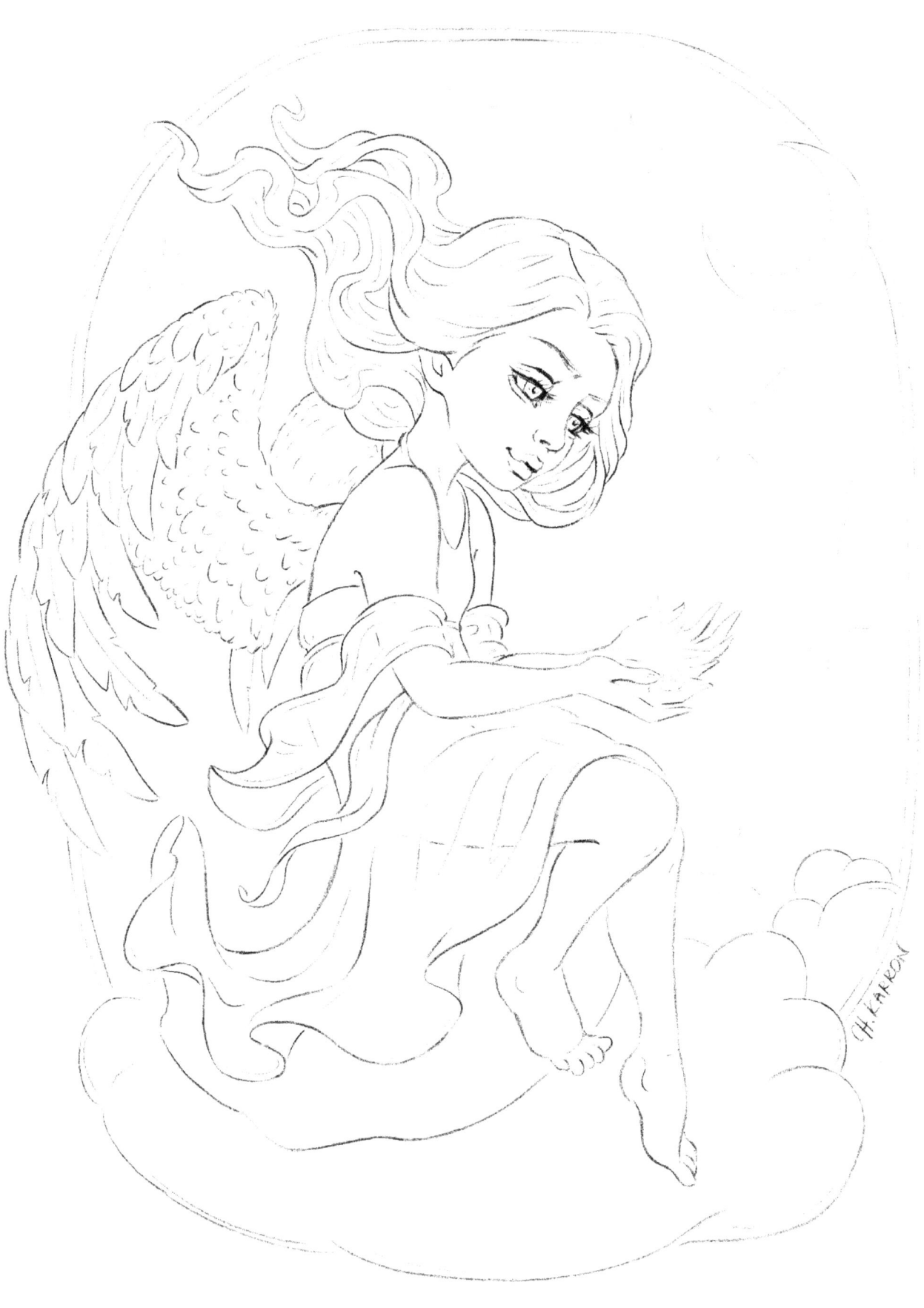

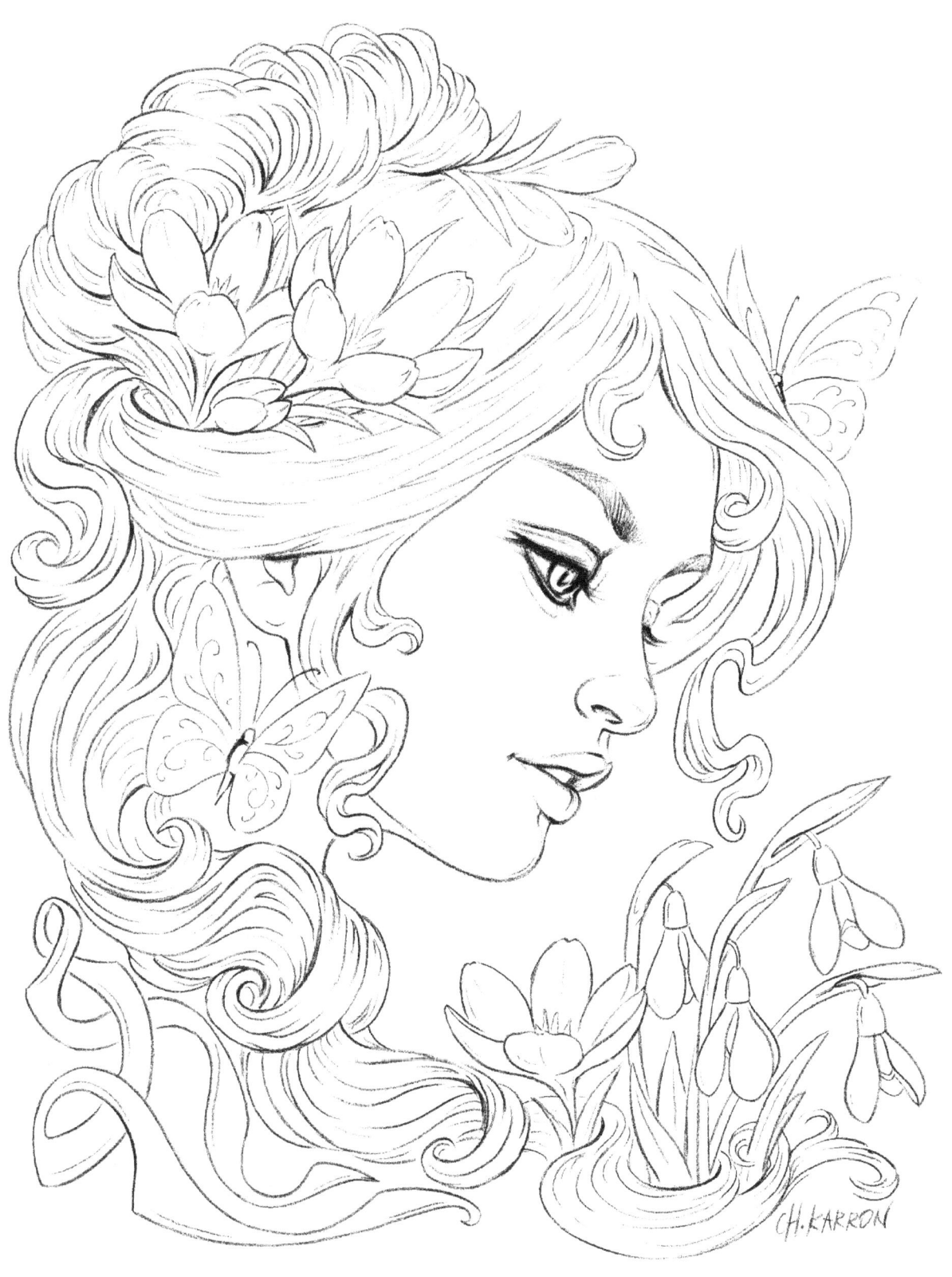

Fairy and Fantasy 3 © Christine Karron

Spring Awakening

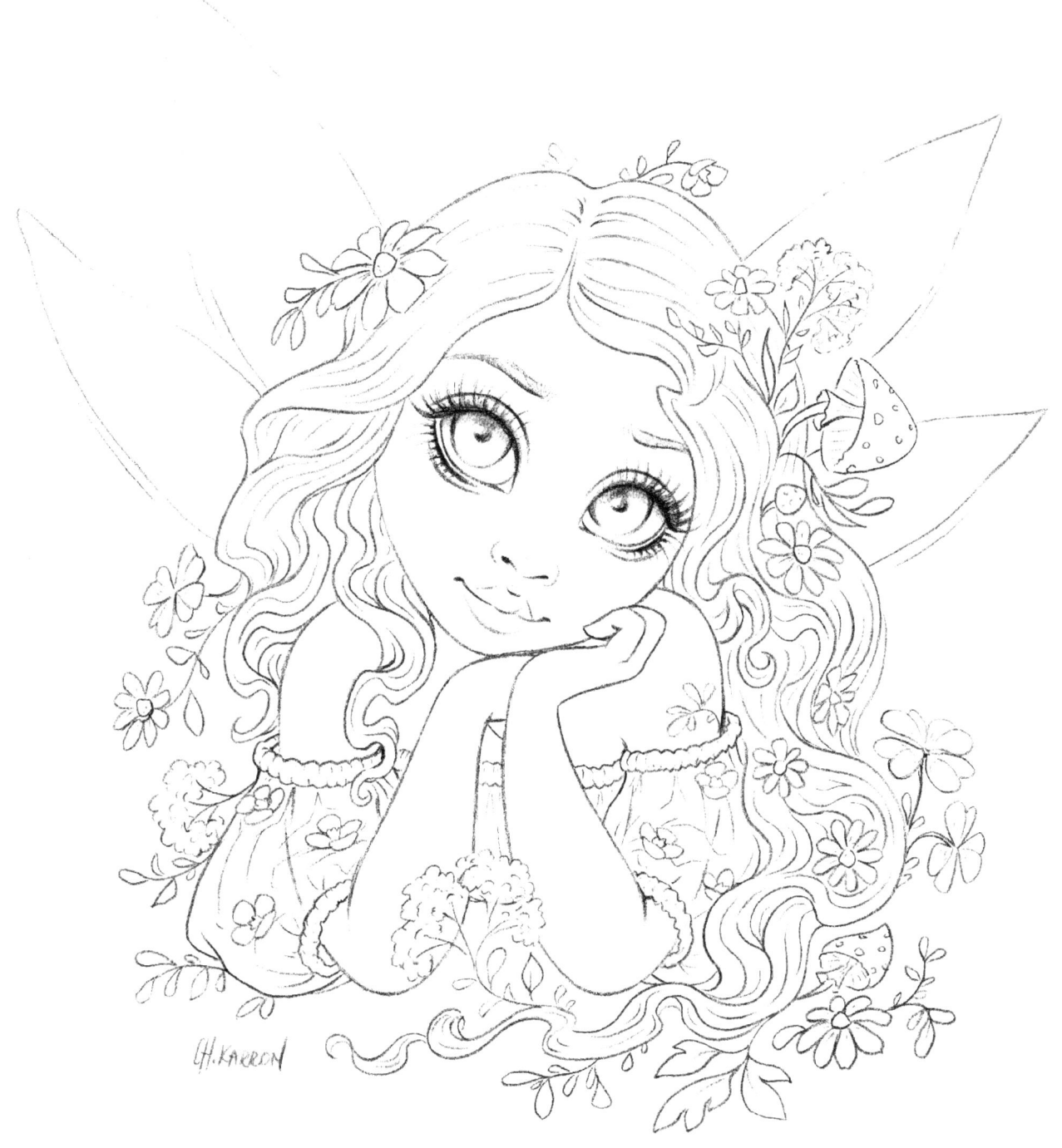

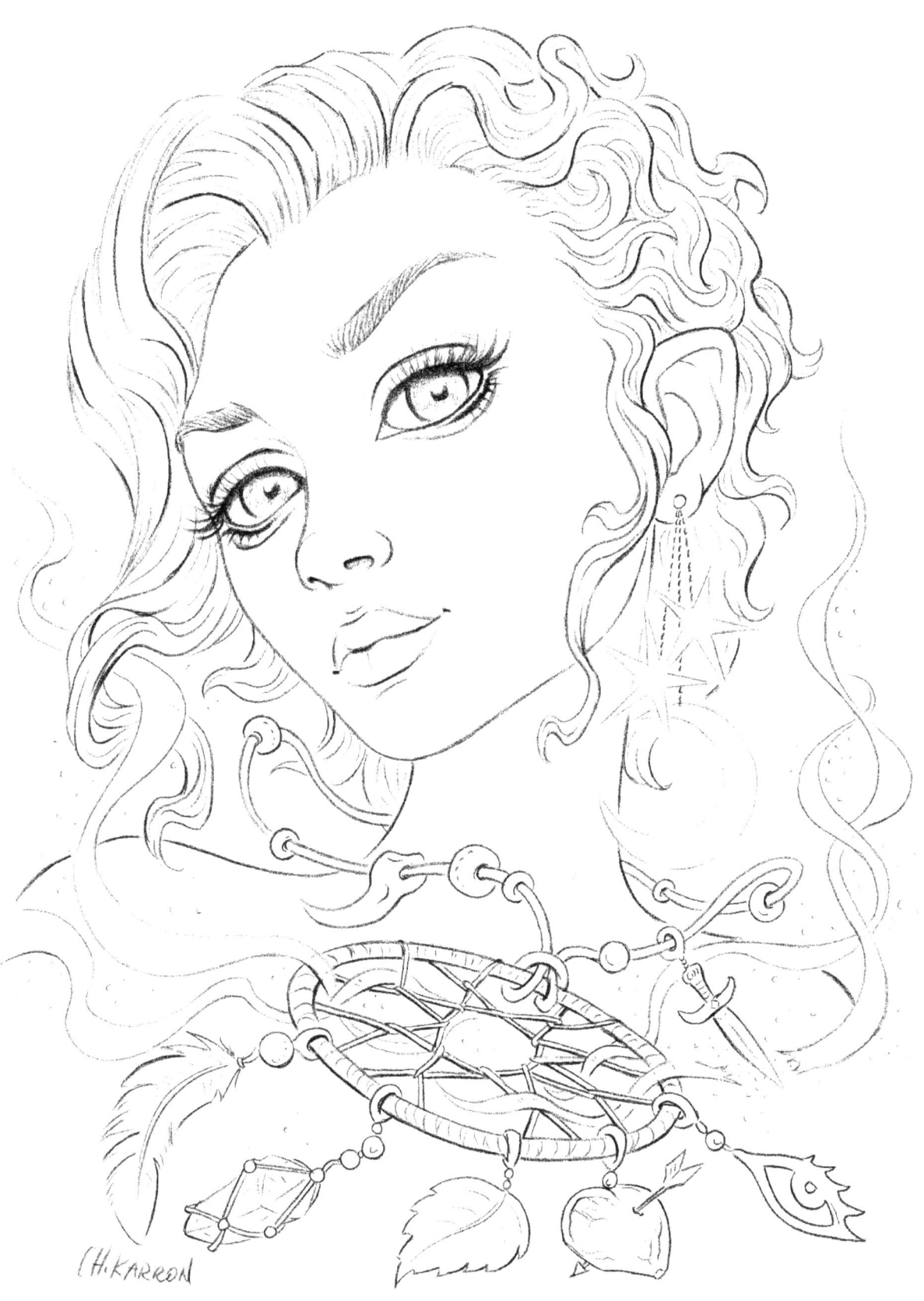

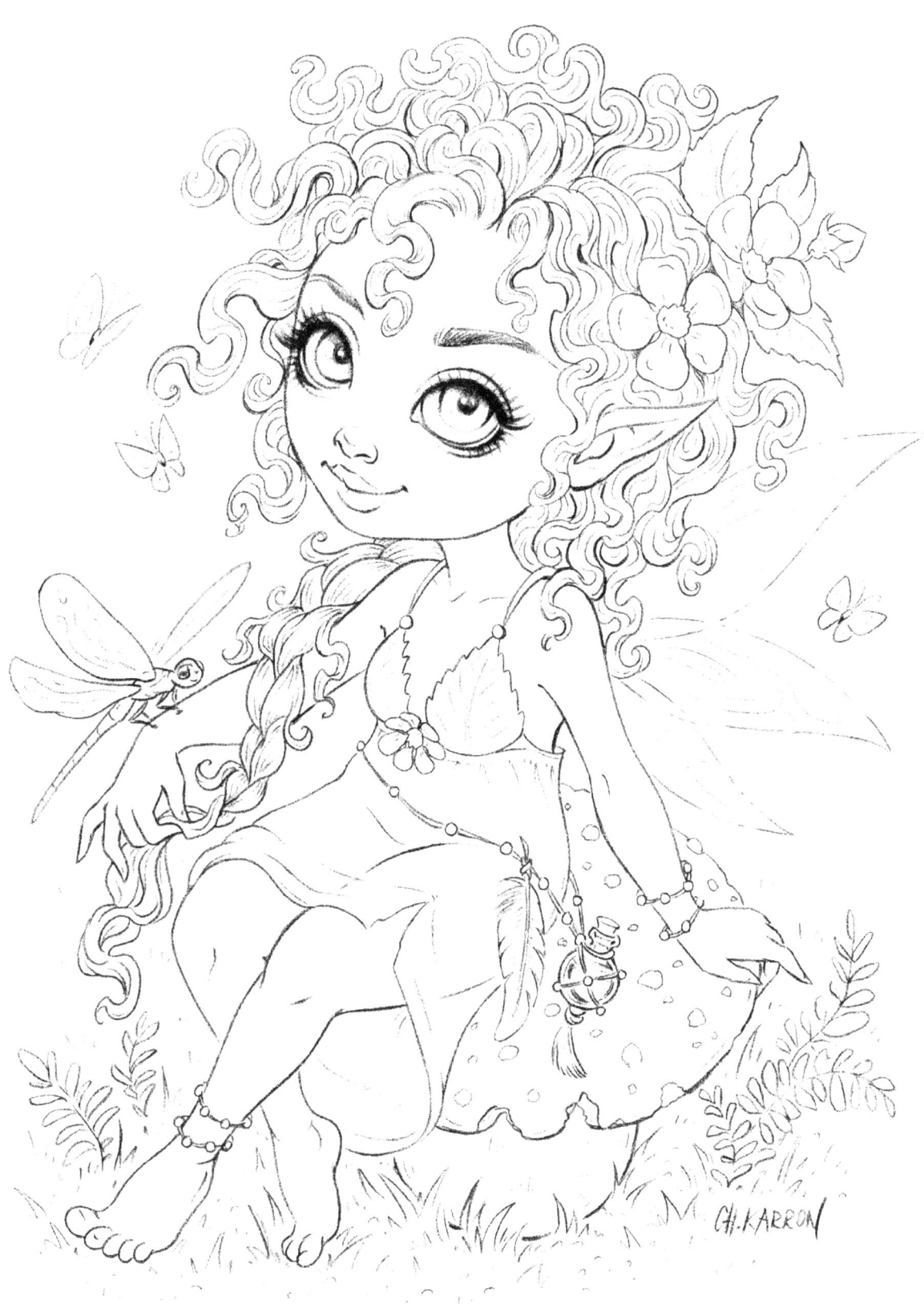

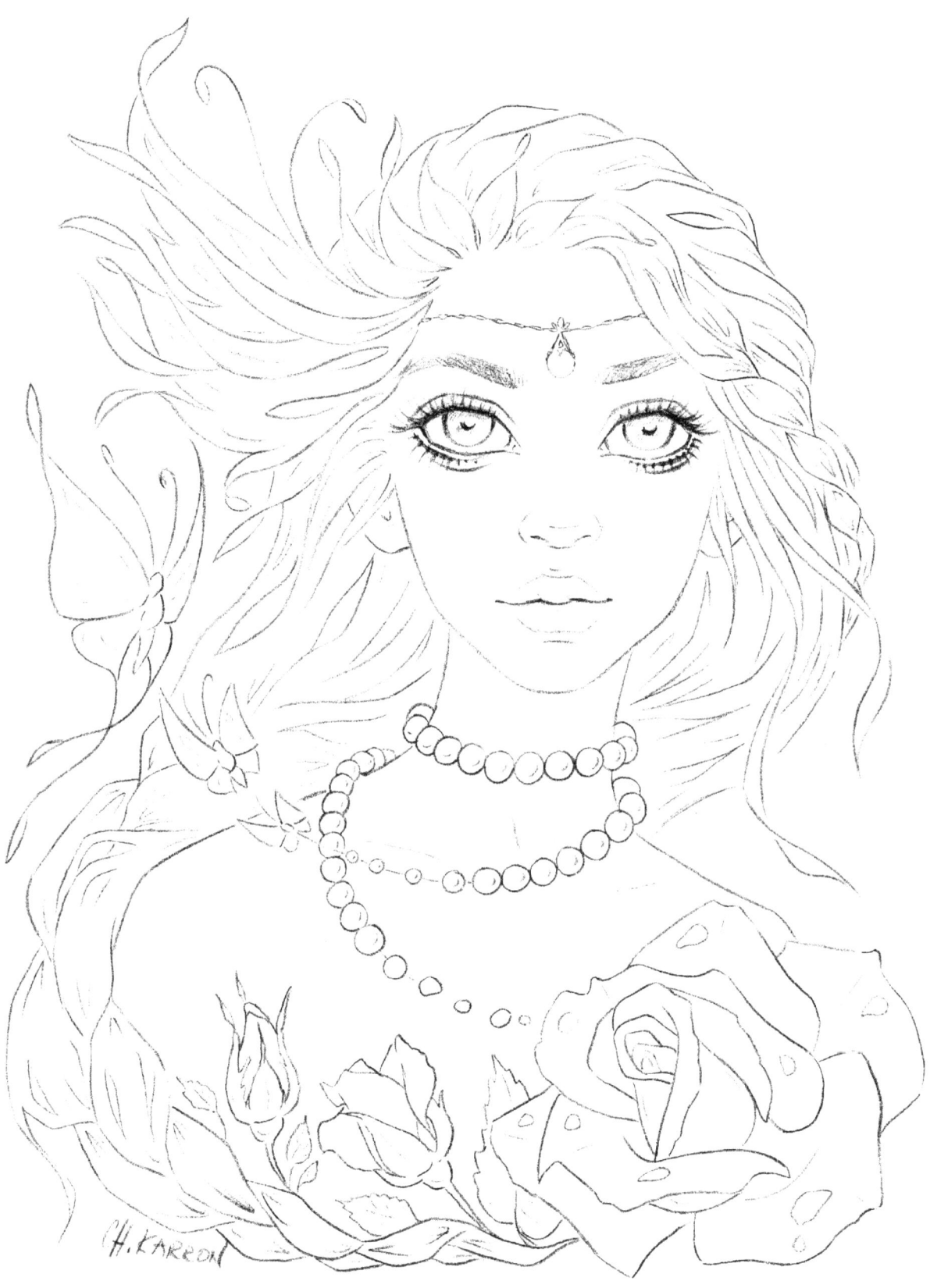

Fairy and Fantasy 3 © Christine Karron Pearls of Life

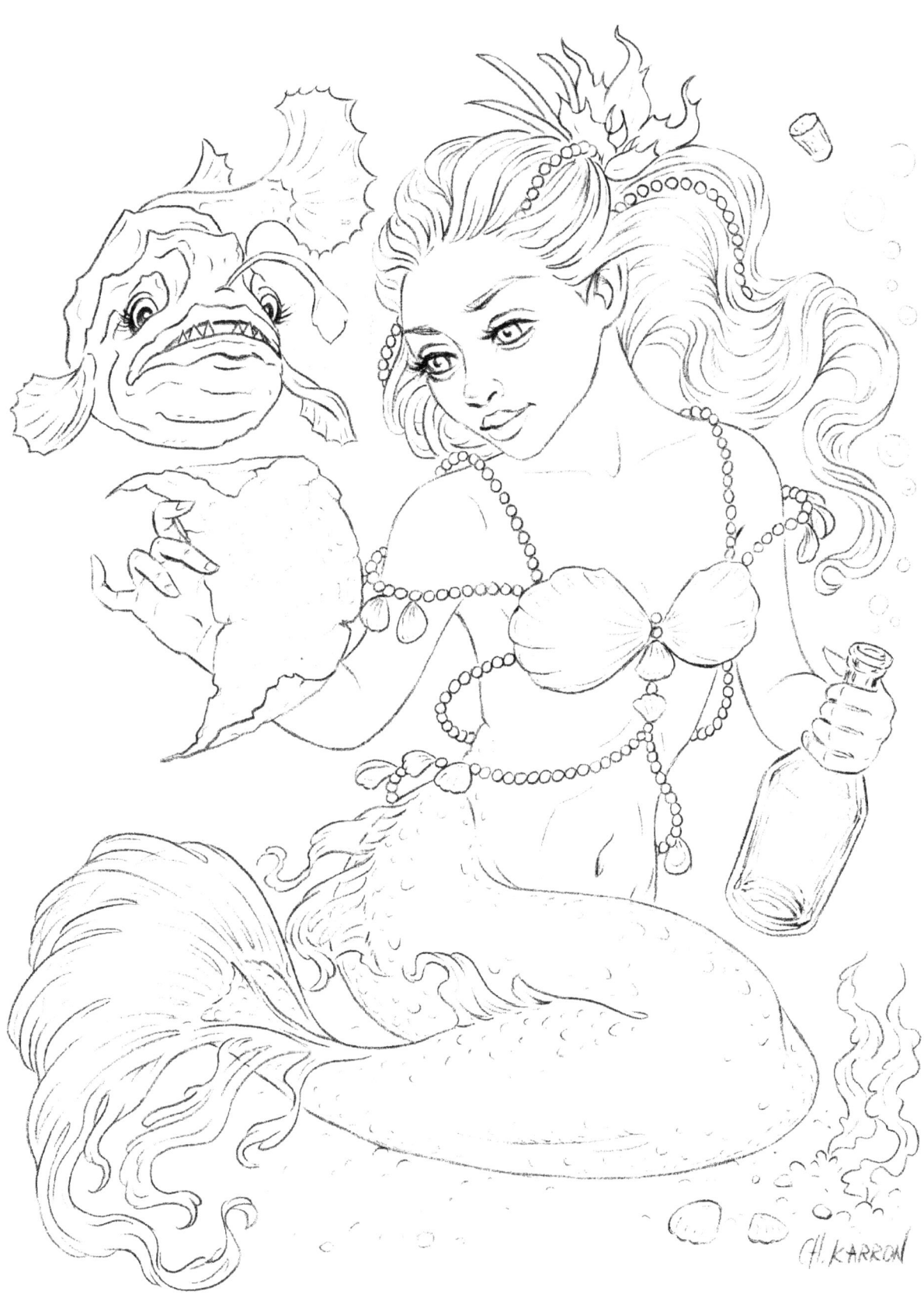

Fairy and Fantasy 3 © Christine Karron   Message in the Bottle

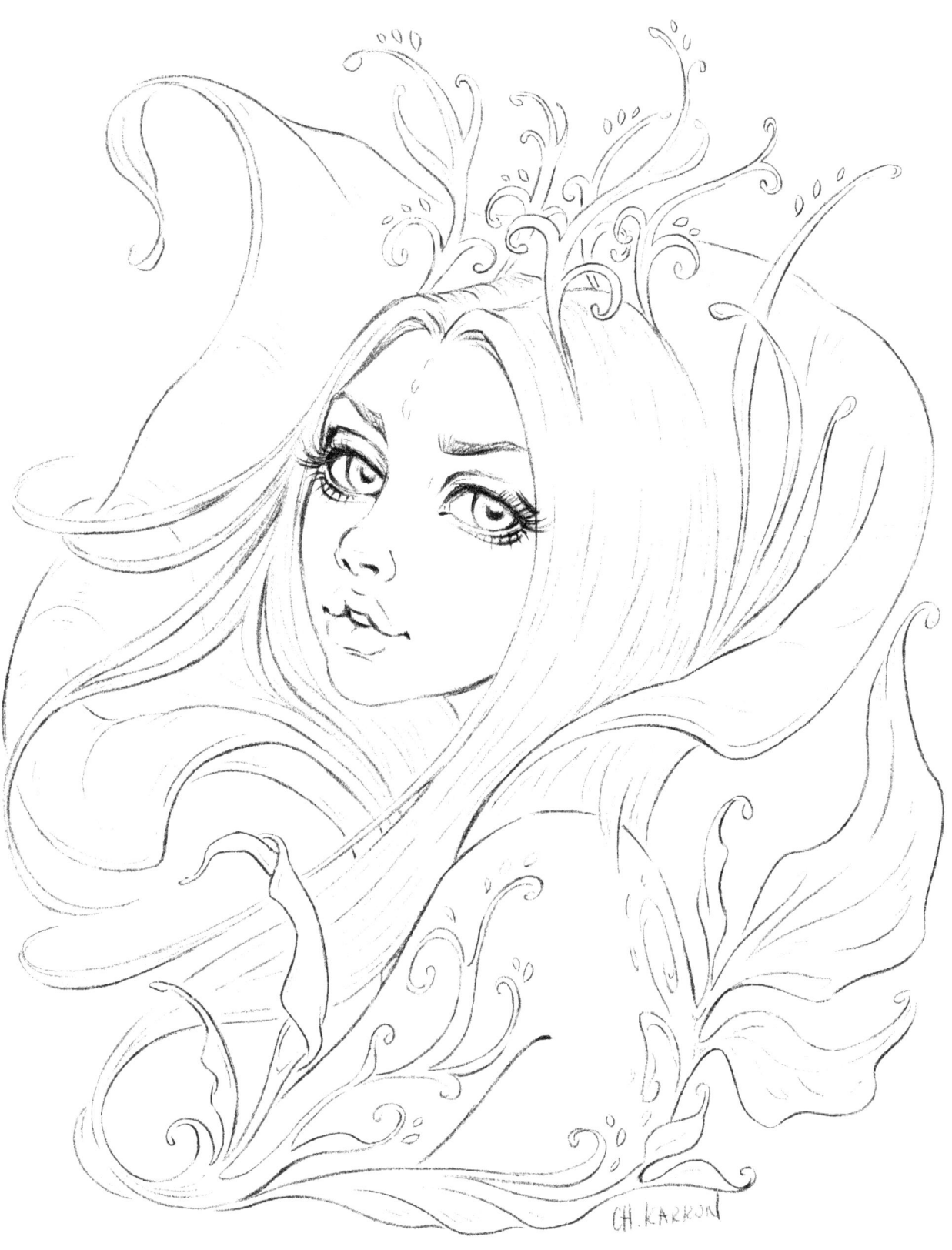

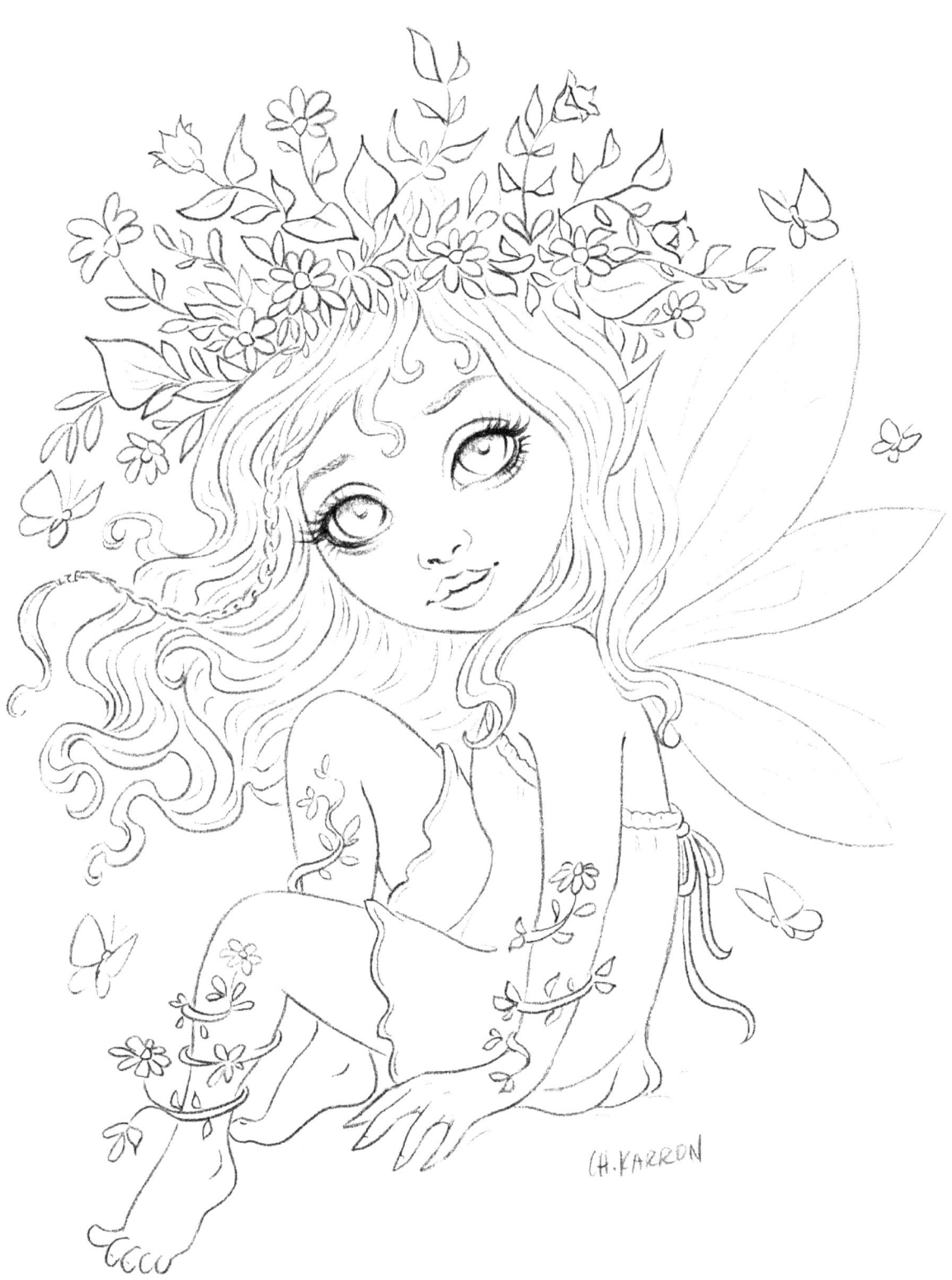

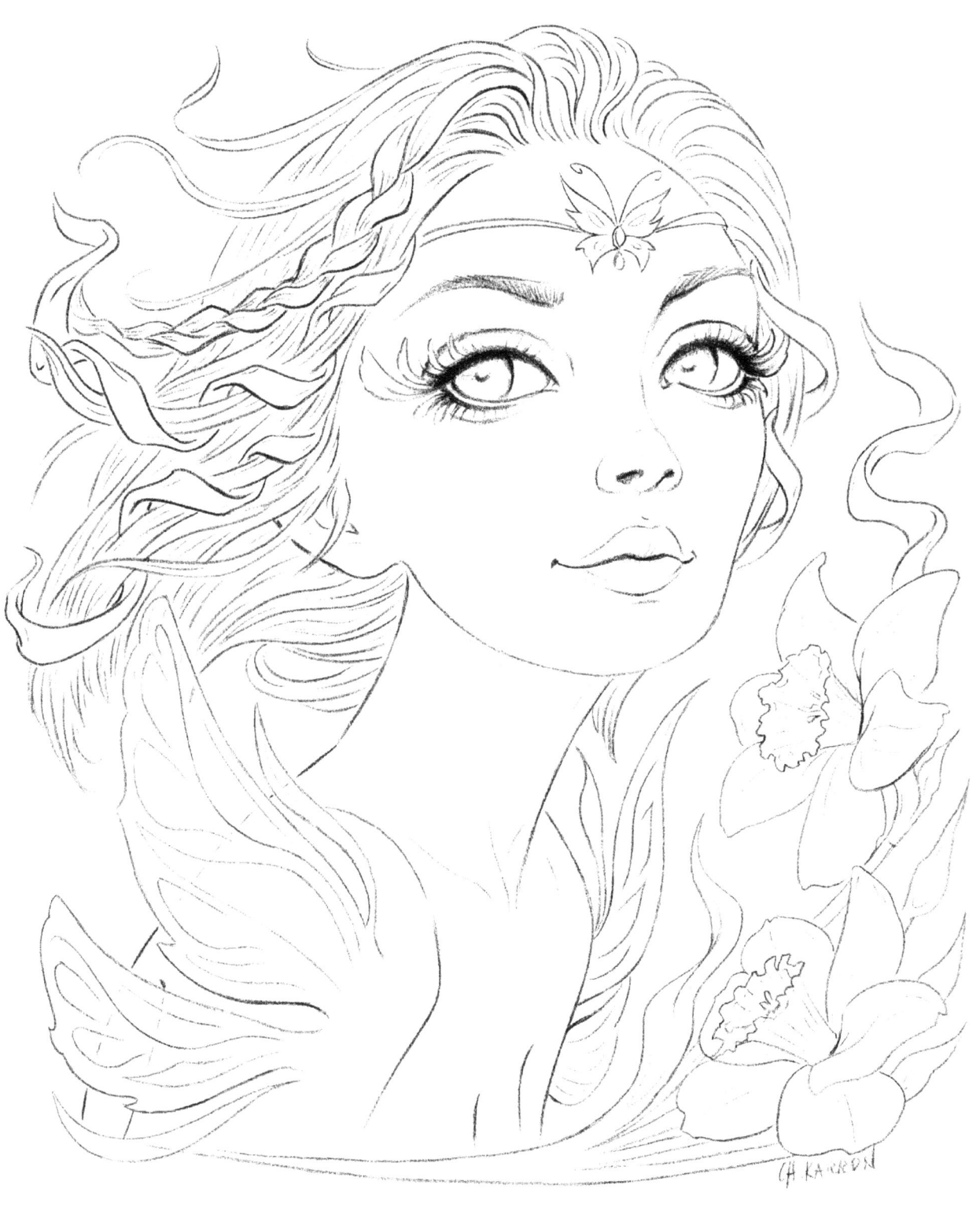

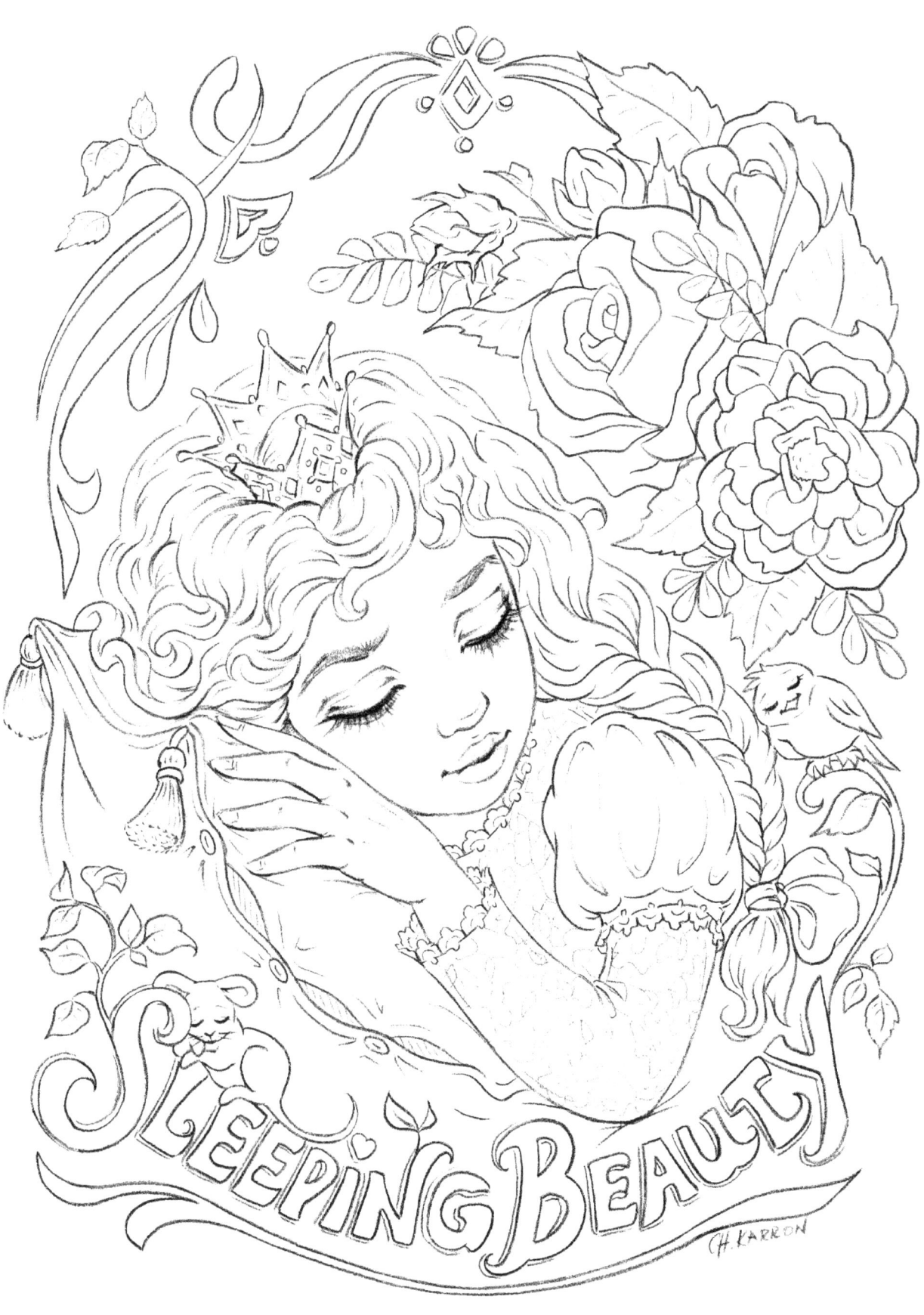

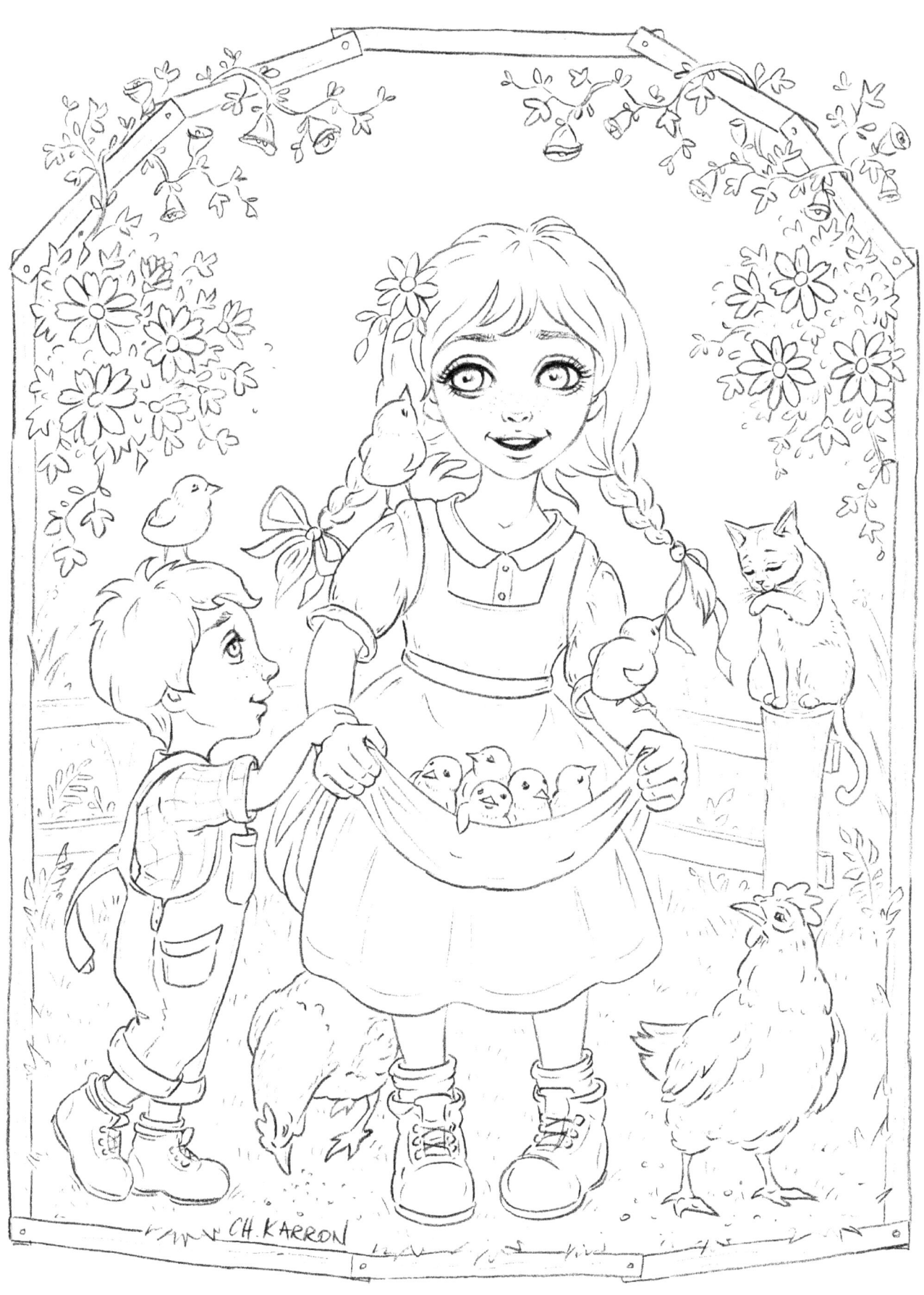

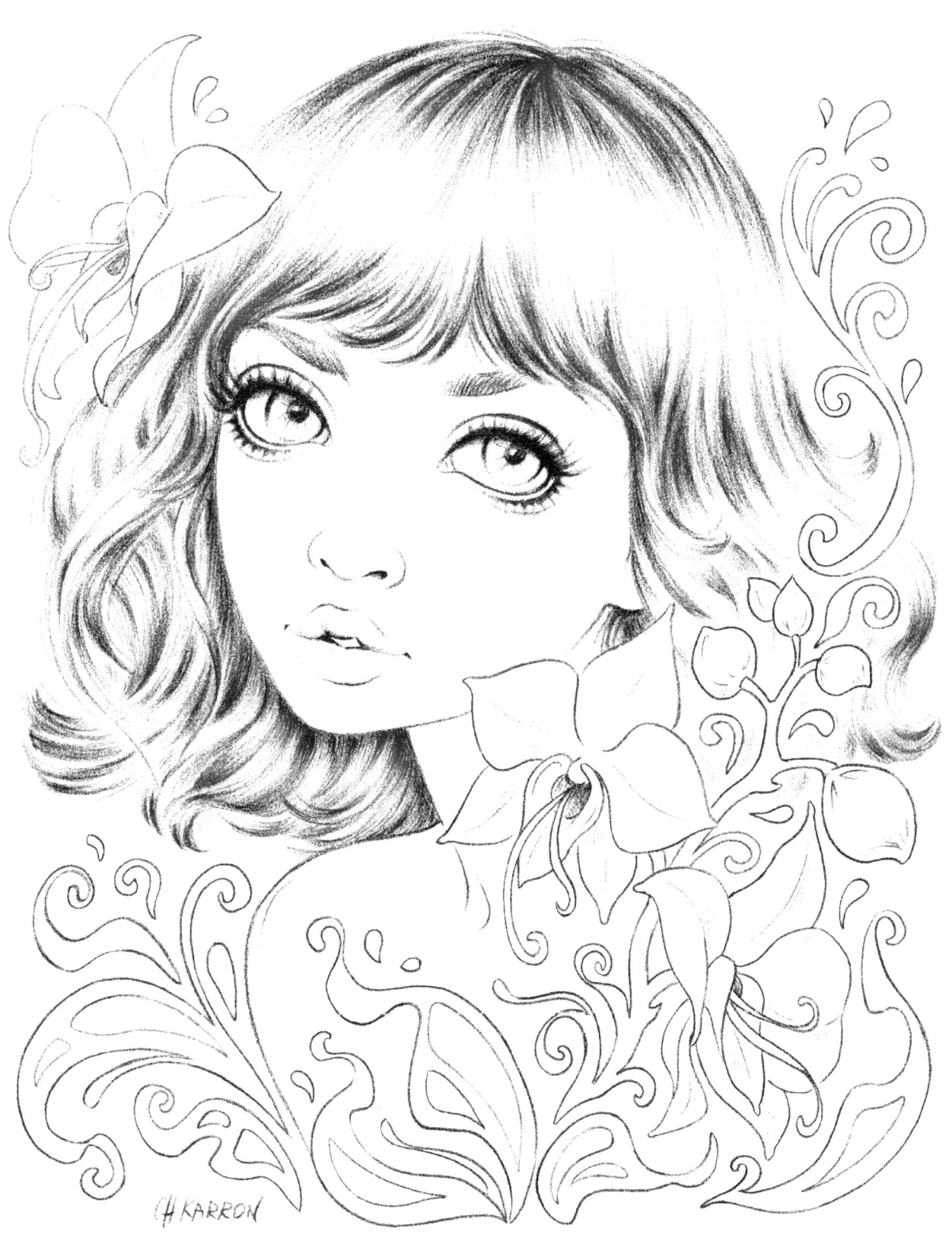

Fairy and Fantasy 3 © Christine Karron	Orchid Dream

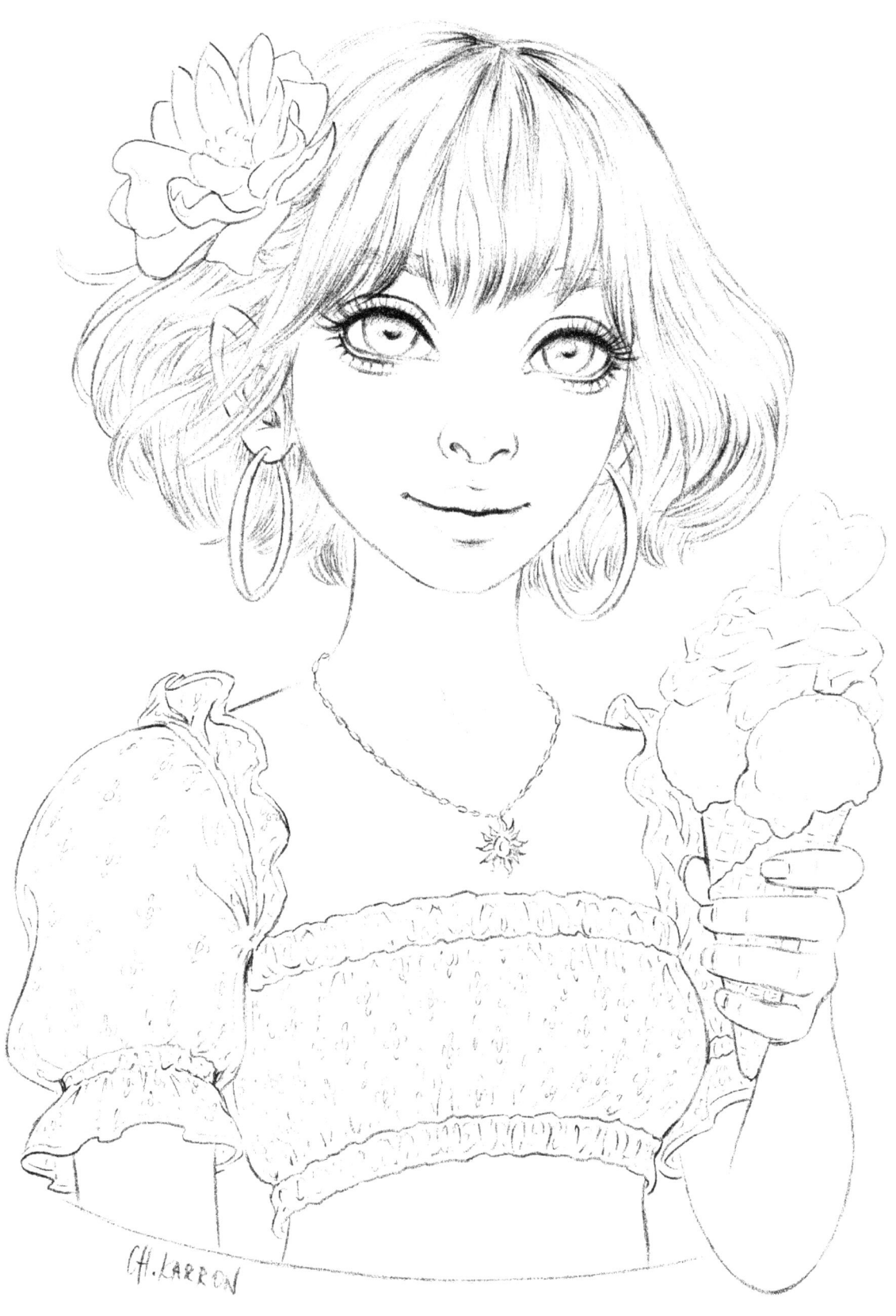

Fairy and Fantasy 3 © Christine Karron Joys of Summer

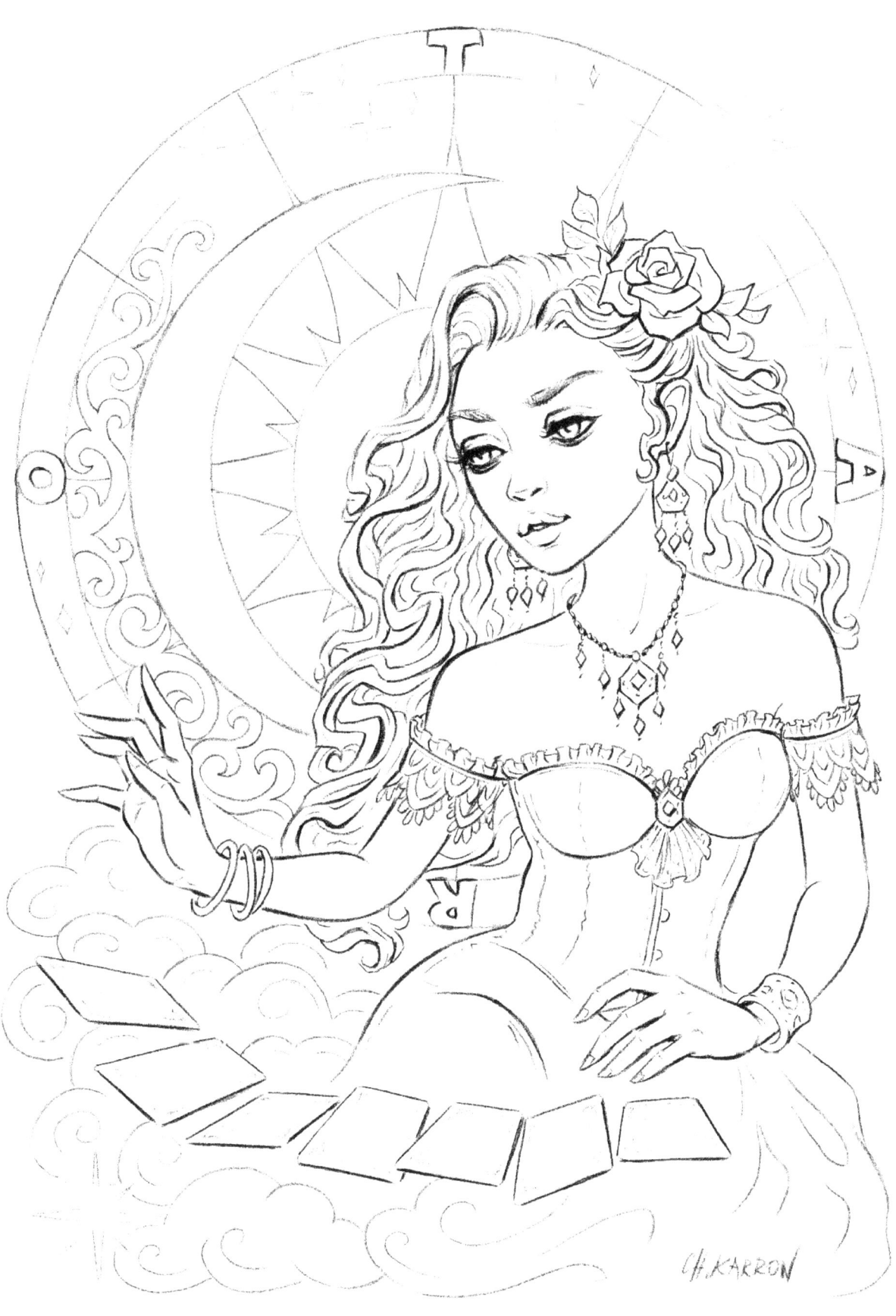

Fairy and Fantasy 3 © Christine Karron Tarot Reader

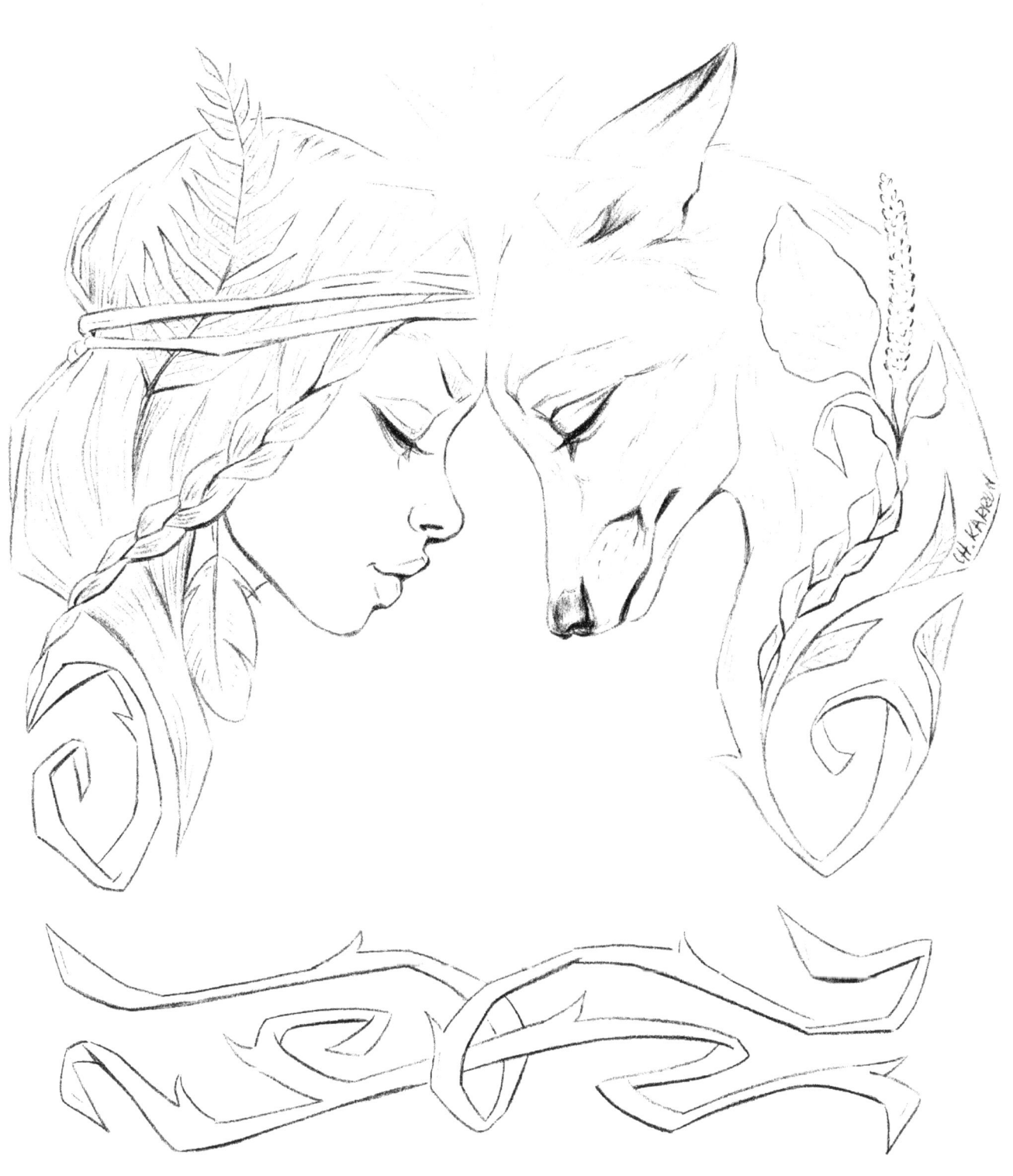

Also available:

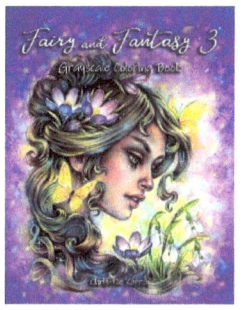 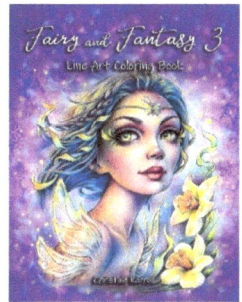 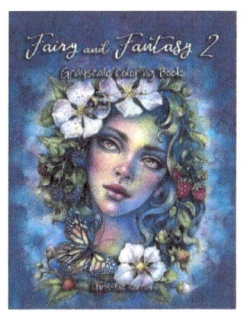 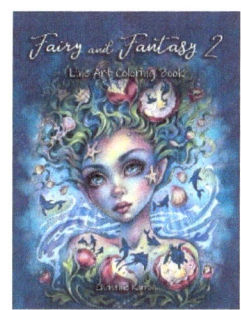

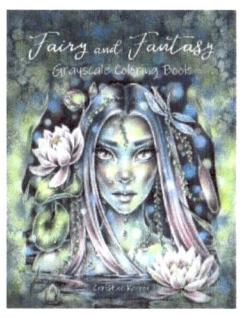 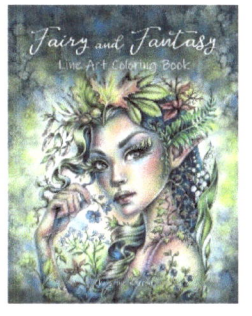 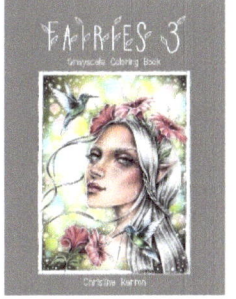 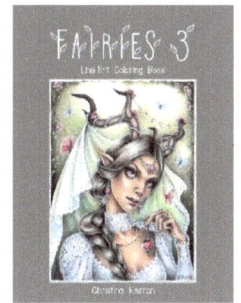

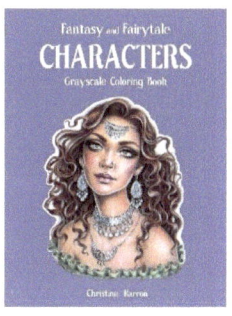 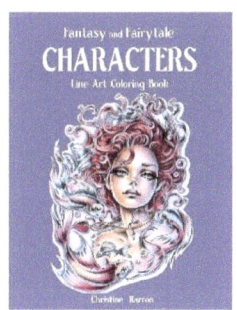 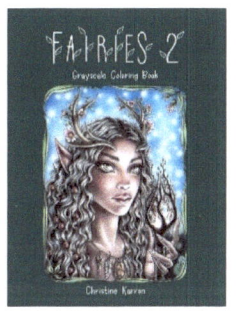 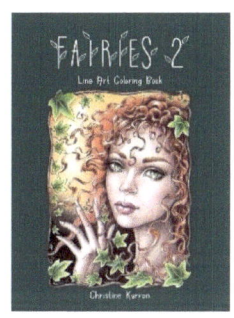

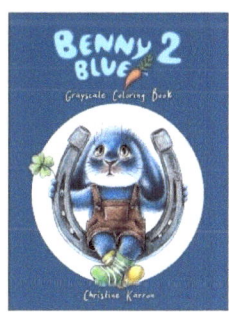 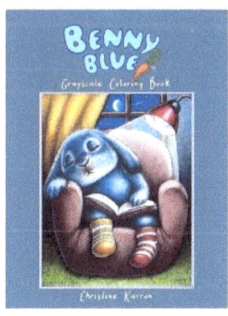 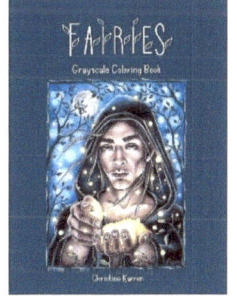 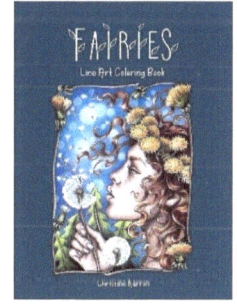

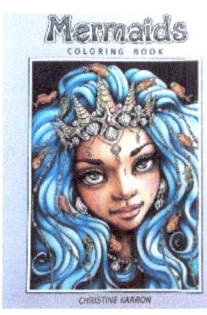 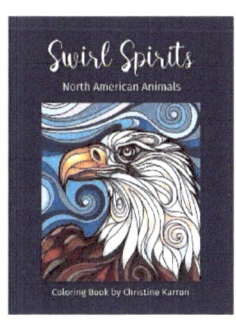 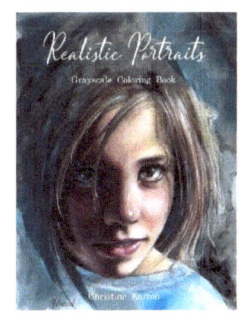

***

*Christine Karron is a Canadian artist and illustrator.
More info at www.chkarron.com*

Facebook:
Christine Karron Art and illustration

Facebook coloring group:
Christine Karron Coloring Collection Fan Group

Instagram: @chkarron

YouTube: Christine Karron

Etsy shop: Christine Karron
Printable digital coloring page downloads

If sharing colored images online, please credit the artist
Christine Karron. You can use hashtags
#christinekarron and #chkarron
Please DO NOT share or post uncolored versions of
the images from this book on Facebook,
Pinterest or any other sharing sites online.

www.chkarron.com

www.ingramcontent.com/pod-product-compliance
Lightning Source LLC
Chambersburg PA
CBHW051208220526
45473CB00003B/951